CAPYBARAS

by Martha E. H. Rustad

PEBBLE
a capstone imprint

Pebble Explore is published by Pebble, an imprint of Capstone.
1710 Roe Crest Drive
North Mankato, Minnesota 56003
www.capstonepub.com

Library of Congress Cataloging-in-Publication data is available on the Library of Congress website.
ISBN 978-1-9771-2313-8 (library binding)
ISBN 978-1-9771-2647-4 (paperback)
ISBN 978-1-9771-2321-3 (eBook PDF)

Summary: Text describes capybaras, including where they live, their bodies, what they do, and dangers to capybaras.

Image Credits
Capstone Press, 8; Newscom: Jurgen & Christine Sohns/FLPA imageBROKER, 19; Shutterstock: buteo, 1, 5, 15, Cheewin Blue, 20, Erwin Widmer, 10, EvergreenPlanet, 13, Jaboticaba Fotos, 11, Kylie Nicholson, Cover, LeanneB, 16, Massis, 24, N_FUJITA, 14, Natalia Kuzmina, top 27, Nazzu, 9, Ondrej Prosicky, 23, Pertfoto, 6, RPBaiao, 4, Seokhee Kim, bottom 27, Uwe Bergwitz, 25, Zaruba Ondrej, 7

Editorial Credits
Editor: Hank Musolf; Designer: Dina Her; Media Researcher: Morgan Walters; Production Specialist: Tori Abraham

All internet sites appearing in back matter were available and accurate when this book was sent to press.

Printed in the United States of America.
PA117

Table of Contents

Words in **bold** are in the glossary.

Amazing Capybaras

An animal makes a loud sound. Bark! It swims underwater.

Brown fur covers its body. Short ears lie back on its head. It has no tail.

What is it? A capybara!

A capybara is a kind of animal called a **rodent**. They are the biggest rodents in the world. They have long front teeth that grow all their lives.

Capybaras, or capies, are related to beavers. But beavers have long tails. Capybaras have almost no tail. Beavers and capybaras also live in different parts of the world.

Where Capybaras Live

Capybaras live in Central and South America. They live in **rain forests**. These hot, wet forests have many trees. Capybaras are found in grasslands and normal forests too.

Capybaras Range Map

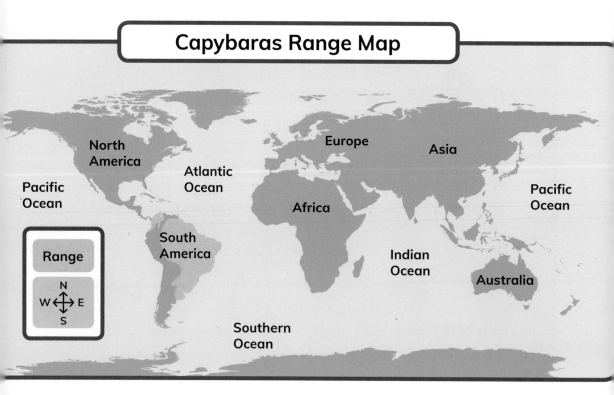

North America

Europe

Asia

Atlantic Ocean

Pacific Ocean

Pacific Ocean

Africa

Range

South America

Indian Ocean

N
W ⟵✛⟶ E
S

Australia

Southern Ocean

Capies spend time in swamps and marshes. They always live near water. They hide under the water if danger comes near. They can hold their breath as long as five minutes. Capybaras rest in mud. This helps them keep cool.

A group, or **herd**, of capies walks over an area of land. This land is called a **territory**. It can be as big as 25 acres (10 hectares). They keep other capybaras out.

Capybaras move around at different times of the year. During the rainy time, grasslands flood. The herds spread out. In the dry time, capies follow rivers and lakes. They share water with other herds.

Capybara Bodies

Capybaras have strong, heavy bodies. They have square heads. Small capies weigh about 80 pounds (36 kilograms). Large ones weigh about 150 pounds (68 kg). That is as much as an adult person!

Capybaras stretch almost 5 feet (150 centimeters) long. They are about 2 feet (60 cm) tall at their shoulders.

Brown fur covers capybaras. The hairs are long and stiff. Their fur dries quickly out of the water.

Capies have four toes on their front paws. They have three toes on their back paws. Skin stretches between their toes. These **webbed feet** help them swim.

A capy's front legs are shorter than their back legs. They sometimes hop on land. Speedy capybaras can run up to 22 miles (35 kilometers) per hour.

The front teeth of a capybara never stop growing. Chewing on bark and branches wears down their teeth. Capybaras chew and chew all day.

A bump sits on top of a capybara's nose. It is called a **morillo**. Males have large morillos. A capybara rubs its morillo on plants. This leaves a smell behind. It tells other animals to stay away. This helps keep the land where the herd lives safe.

Eating and Drinking

In the morning and evening, capybaras look for food. They eat up to 8 pounds (3.6 kg) of food each day. They usually eat water plants. A capybara's diet changes in dry weather. Then they eat dry reeds, grain, melons, and sugar cane.

The grasses that capybaras eat have a lot of **fiber**. They are hard to break down, or **digest**. Capybaras deal with this in two ways. Each morning, capybaras eat their own poop. This lets them digest their food twice. Capybaras also spit up and rechew food.

Baby capybaras drink milk from their mother's bodies. When they are just a few days old, they start eating grasses.

What Capybaras Do

A capybara's day starts early. Before the sun is up, capybaras find food. They nibble on grasses and leaves.

During the day, capybaras look for places to stay cool and safe. **Predators** hunt capybaras. Capybaras stay safe from them by hiding. They might stay hidden all day. They make beds in thick plants.

The sun sets. Capybaras come out from hiding. They look around for danger. Capybaras might stay up all night eating.

Capybaras live in family groups.
About 20 animals live together in a
herd. When herds share water, up to
100 capies might live together.

One male capybara leads a herd. Females mate with him. After four months, a litter of three to eight pups is born. A female has about one litter each year.

Pups can stand up and walk right away. Pups stay with their herd for about a year. Adults keep them safe from predators. Capies usually live 8-10 years.

Dangers to Capybaras

Many predators hunt capybaras. Some kinds of snakes eat them. Jaguars and pumas are big cats that hunt capybaras. Large reptiles called **caimans** snap at swimming capybaras. Eagles grab at pups.

People sometimes hunt capybaras. Some places outlaw hunting these animals.

Humans also move into areas where capybaras live. People cut down trees to grow crops. This leaves fewer forests for capybaras to live in.

Many people are working to protect rain forests. They plant trees. Farmers learn new ways of growing crops. This means capybaras can stay in the places where they live.

Fast Facts

Name: capybara

Habitat: grasslands, rain forests, marshes, and swamps near water

Where in the World: Central and South America

Food: water plants, grasses, melons, reeds, grains

Predators: jaguars, pumas, caimans, snakes, eagles

Life span: 8 to 10 years

Glossary

caiman (KAY-muhn)—a reptile similar to an alligator

digest (dy-GEST)—to move food through the body and draw minerals from it

fiber (FY-buhr)—part of food that is hard for the body to break down and get nutrition from

herd (HURD)—a group of animals that lives together

morillo (mohr-ILL-oh)—a bump on top of a capybara's nose; capies rub this scent gland on plants to mark their territory

predator (PRED-uh-tor)—an animal that hunts other animals for food

rain forest (RAYN FOR-ist)—an area of thick trees where lots of rain falls

rodent (ROHD-uhnt)—a mammal with long front teeth used for gnawing

territory (TER-uh-tor-ee)—an area where a group of animals lives

webbed feet (WEBD FEET)—feet with wide flaps of skin between the toes; this helps animals swim better

Read More

Koestler-Grack, Rachel. *Capybaras*. Minneapolis: Bellwether Media, 2019.

Lunis, Natalie. *Capybara: The World's Largest Rodent*. New York: Bearport Pub, 2019.

Niver, Heather M. Moore. *Capybaras After Dark*. New York: Enslow Publishing, 2017.

Internet Sites

A Capybara Family's Day at Play
safeyoutube.net/w/TtGq

Capybara
www.chesterzoo.org/our-zoo/animals/capybara/

Fun Facts about Cute Animals: Capybara Edition
www.cbc.ca/kidscbc2/the-feed/fun-facts-about-cute-animals-capybara-edition

Index